absence

absence
in the palms of my hands
& other poems

by
asha bandele

Harlem River Press
NEW YORK
& LONDON

Published for Harlem River Press
by Writers and Readers Publishing, Inc.
P. O. Box 461, Village Station
New York, NY 10014

Writers and Readers Limited
2a Britannia Row
London N1 8QH

Editor: Patricia A. Allen
Cover Design: Terrie Dunkelberger
Cover Photograph © 1999: Robert Lee Hughie
Book Design: Tenth Avenue Editions, Inc.,
    Clive Giboire & Suzanne Cobban

Library of Congress Cataloging-in-Publication Data
Bandele, Asha
Absence in the palms of my hands & other poems / by asha bandele.
p.   cm.
ISBN 0-86316-013-1 (pbk.)
I. Title.
PS3552.A47527A63   1996
811'.54--dc20   96-20896
                                                 CIP

Manufactured in the United States of America

Some of these poems have also recently appeared in
In the Tradition; Aloud, In Defense of Mumia,
and in *Excursos* and *Konceptualizations* magazines.

for Audre Lorde,

who admonished us that *we are the offspring of slaves and our mother
was a princess in darkness* /& Audre Lorde, who reached, even when she
didn't have to, even when she was tired, and even to me, long before i
had idea what it meant to reach back / i love you more today than i
did yesterday /& i know they say u can't kill a spirit so you are & always
will be here/& in a way i know that/still/i miss your voice
your scolding/& you just
you alla you real real
bad.

contents

acknowledgment must be made to...

the Holy spirit / who directs & blesses us all & who gave me /mommy-n-daddy/ab/warren/lauren/peter/ mk /tkalla-grand ave & cambridge place/USB all of us/baba/hb/jalil/nuh/ doc/ mr. b/ras/ kevin powell/ medina/asale/ c.bell/imani/ april/goapele/noah/tanaquil/safiya/ errol/ maulana/willie /m2/ rt/ marcelle/ namane/ azibuke/ keba/ willpower/ laila/THE UPPER ROOM/mr. bilal/ brothershine/dejah/michele /tina/even u t.c.-a shout out to say i remember how it wuz once/yeah lorena monifa dream mxg/thomas p./hatem/stations - the whole crew /sapphire/hunter college /elaine equi/ elaine edelman / aya /jasiri/ israel / kian / rabbi /cliff j/veb/the blackarts movements 1920s–1960s / a.k./wanjiku/zayid/big e. & devorah & the whole KONCEPTS concept (oaktown representin)/eric kikanza rita /theo / emilio/ miss richardson/ marjorie/ mujah / ayanna/ dhameera/ nisa /anna s./ muntu /sam /joseph r./donna w. / miss radcliff from washington irving hs u too/the brothers at nap. 1991-3/the people whose faces watched/in secret/ whose words i heard long after/ & rashid / & rashid again /& i don't know how 2 do it / say what i mean / but fannie lou hamer said we can't never forget where we came from & gotta praise all the bridges that carried us over /so what i mean is u who gave & is giving me life & reason & movement & thought & possibility & inspiration always & always/ i love you all even the all i don't see no more/ my love didn't ever fade tho i didn't always have what it took 2 say it/show it each time i needed 2 / 2 each of u/ yr meaning could never be vanished / even who i failed to mention/ or have forget cuz its been so long/ u exist forever/ in the best of me/be u /
asante sana

& 4 the love-n-labor
the belief & beauty
of marie brown glenn thompson patricia allen deborah dyson
& all the staff of writers & readers/harlem river press
there are no words

absence

in the palms of my hands

& other poems

preface

habeus corpus is a legal entitlement

*for the men at eastern correctional facility who felt
i should not include curses in my poetry*

1.

this poem is a writ of habeus corpus meaning
get yo/hands off me
b4 i kill you

2.

in america
1 in 21 blkmen will be shot 2 death/being shot
is the leading cause of death
4 blkmen aged 15 to 24
u wanna hear more?
had u been in vietnam during the war
u were more likely to survive than u are today
if you're blk / male / & btwn 15 & 25
&
u
ask
me

why i curse & rage & sound obscene
explain whatchu mean
what is more offensive than the way we live
except perhaps
the way we die
       & this poem is a call out

where are the warriors
where are the truth tellers
where are the fearless dragons
where are the life creators/the life sustainers
the singers of songs of liberation
where are the builders of the nation

where are the war dancers & blkpanthers
the righteous & the mighty
where are the race men
the proud people
the Holy Spirits
the tireless foot soldiers carrying the word
(carry the word soldier)
use the spear & shield & lite
let it shine in the underground tunnels taking us back
way way on back blkpeople   we been gone so long
did we forget
there was life b4 the brandings   the auction blocks   the rapes
(our mommies shredded on the inside/torn by more violations than even
she could count/noooo don't touch my mommy don't hurt my
mommy/daddy please...yet he too was silenced/his mouth stuffed with his
own genitalia)

but b4 this
there was life
came back 2 that
came back blk 2 that
come way on back   *we had been a peaceful people*
                         original east african languages had no
                         words 2 denote possession

                         we had been a correct people
                         known 2 welcome strangers
                         & 2 honor the land
                         & 2 the honor the magic produced by the land
come back blk/magic people
allow no one to replace
the pyramids
with those crack houses & prisons
allow no one
2
replace the pyramids

3.

yo/baby
fuck dat
!!!BANG BANG BLAU BLAU!!!
dats how we livin now
minute 2 minute
& bullet 2 bullet
  *(now the only shorts i takes are the one's that i wear   ain't takin'
  no shorts no mo)**
BLAU BLAU!!!
harder than rock 17 rounds in my glock
is my best friend 2 the muthafuckin end
BLAU BLAU!!!
so
tell
me
how
?
how do i write a poem about life in my city
about racism hatred & the resulting tribal wars
that leave in their wake bloody open sores
swelling prison doors
locking down the daily promise
the 360 degrees
of life / strength
& knowledge

&
someone asked me
why i curse
?
!
u tell me what words sound worse than
starvation
homelessness
oppression
prison
murder

&
greed
what sounds worse than children in need
of safety   love   clothing
housing & healthcare
of education & food
or simply put

> justice
> a
> one
> word
> prayer**

4.

& i wanna write poems that make beauty appear
but 2 do that i gotta write poems that create anger & fear
poems that make us so afraid 4 our lives
we'll finally fight 4 lives
we need poems that straight up
terrorize
all those among us
who worship not children
but gold
we need poetry that breaks the american mold
that tears open at the core all the lies & more
poetry that makes blk/lions roar
freedom!
while building a world safe to live in
a world where blk/dead & 16
is no longer a given
we need poetry that screams
this cracka's a deadly muthafucka & there ain't no reason we got 2 go out
& go out like suckers
& 4 my people on the inside
what can be said that sounds nice or pretty
about any so-called correctional facility
the path travelled that brought each one of us here
is a long train of abuses & a trail of tears***

& this poet feels war-torn with blood in my eyes
my throat is scratched raw with desperate cries

        retribution! 4 john kelly killed the last day of '91
        (he was blk they was wite that's the only reason)
        retribution! 4 more people than i ever could mention
        including prisoners & the long years of detention

if we want liberation
we gotta stand firm & show it
& never again tell any blk/poet
to play words games
& put harsh language on ice
& somehow make our genocide
sound nice.

*sung by A Tribe Called Quest
**sung by Ziggy Marley
***from the American Declaration of Independence

chapter one

the homegirl in us

4 donna (during the audre years)

fear;
     & i can't loosen my own brown hands
     wrapped round my own brown throat
     this feeling of being born/living
     with the cord tightening on my neck   i
                                             can't
                                         breathe   most times

     i can't breathe

it's real;
     i am a blkwoman
     this is america
     i live outside my own life
     in an internal state of war
     dreaming of what it would be like
     2 be
     at peace

this legacy of silence;
     when we met i had no language
no way 2 call 2 you

     but you said
     you are a blkwoman   this is america
     each chance you get 2 speak
     might be your last

but my words have been used against me
donna
by those i loved the most
getting 2 the place where i can at last feel safe
is the most dangerous journey
of all
     you were the first person 2 see beyond differences
     & tell me all my words
     were valid

how will we finally be able 2 focus our blkwoman selves
on what we need
2 survive
?

how will we learn 2 support ourselves outside of therapy
& despair
?
when will we learn 2 move as a whole
?

when will we learn
2
speak
?

absence in the palms of my hands

for audre lorde

i will eat the last signs of my weakness
remove the scars of childhood wars*

i made you this promise as
humble as mary washing the feet of her savior

it was an unsteady may afternoon &
we were standing in the doorway of the home you had adopted
you left me there with
your head raised and still dreadlocked walking
toward the beginnings of your death
i didn't say i'd never *take the chemo* you told me
& though i know we must have spoken after this day
these are the last words i ever remember hearing from
you

audre
i learned to face the complexity of living watching you
face the complexity of dying
   never do it on your knees never do it with your back turned
   never do it with your eyes
low

i learned dialectics watching you at war
a defiant soldier for peace against the serenade of violence
inside & outside
your body   a mighty oak refusing
to be scorched in silence

these days
in the face of necessary battles i know i must
never forget the warnings of my woman's flesh
*nor lose the terror that keeps me brave**
but this morning your memory informs my tears
thick & isolated
unable to rest
it has been two years now but
death does not know time and

your absence aches in the palms of my hands
but i am also angry

i curse the disease because cancer is not natural
nor the act of an unforgiving God
crossing the world we once shared
i see
poison passed off as food   water   air   as
good earth upon which we may live or clear out
the next rainforest to make room for a grinning clown
& hamburger stand

the   whole   world
is being nourished on big macs & radon
staring westward at hollywood for daily salvation
& we do not understand our 5 year olds
when their eyes melt
& they do not scream only
shrug

in the solitude of my writing i place
your poetry around me like a makeshift altar
& pray my generation of poet-historians
will abandon any urge toward the mirage of relevance created 'cause
WE BLEW UP THE SPOT YO!
in the urgent hour of now
we need stories beyond shock value whose
focus is transformation
or at least the prayer that
we will write no words we will not want spoken out of
the mouths of our children

that we will owe nothing we cannot repay.*

from "Solstice" by Audre Lorde (in Black Unicorn)*

last poem at 27

i guess i'd rather watch jeopardy
or wheel of fortune
skip to the comics section
check the far side
scan my astrology

it doesn't really matter

i'd rather complain to my mother
murmur to my boyfriend
debate with my girlfriend
re-do my monthly budget
workout
plan a trip home
plan a trip anywhere
i'd rather clean my house
cook
go shopping
re-organize my files
twist my hair
space out
read a book of poems
read a mystery
stare at the mountains posing arrogantly outside my window
watch the lights do a slowdance on lake merritt
sing off key to nina simone
turn the music louder
& dance
yes   *anyday now anyday now i shall be released*
sh-e-e-t   i'd rather
pay the damn phone company
                                i'd rather
reconcile my bank account
                                i'd rather
run stairs   do pushups on my knuckles
anything

but deal with this
thing
that left me
forever 7 years old
split apart
alone
chewing the flesh off my mouth
alone
stumbling over untied shoelaces on an unpaved road
falling backwards thru hell
alone
watching my life
constructed like a bizarre asymmetrical sandcastle
trying to argue down the tide
while the sun blinks

& i'm afraid to write these feelings down
& i'm afraid to not write these feelings down

& i'm afraid everybody's sick of hearing about this
& i'm afraid everybody's waiting for somebody to talk about this

& i think everybody says that the children are the future
but i think nobody believes that the children are the future

which is how the future keeps getting fucked
forced down on its knees
a dick shoved down its throat
crying please
please
don't.

date rape

mirrors crack in the corners of my dreams
i glue pieces of my face onto broken glass & pray in front of wite altars
blue candles burn seven days for peace tranquillity healing
& girl children who stand on line in my soul
holding crystals against their hearts asking
why?

i get high offa sifting my experience thru astrology numerology
& new age feel good brain drain pseudo science
that tastes like answers to questions
the feminist scholar theorized into words
i could not manifest

but i wanna be that woman
the one everybody seems to think i am
strong
like mumia*
pushing deathrow into a confrontation with itself that sounds like
    a heartbeat
beating honor & courage across miles & time

oh mama whatchu gonna do
now you know what your baby girl's been thru

i saw myself caught in the spaces in his teeth
& bent my head between my legs

i saw myself like something between saliva & penetration
& swallowed my mouth

i saw myself scribbled on policeman's note: no humans involved
& believed
Dear God
i
believed

& even tho i said no   i said no more than once
he touched me
& i thought of wire hangers
bacteria
vaginas shredded raw   ripped
like incriminating evidence
that would expose blood squeezed out of nipples
eye sockets
assholes & lungs
& within that madness
i closed my eyes around the quarter moon & sucked acid out of rainclouds
i reached   beyond knowing
for staccato breath
hydrochloric air   anything not to be there
not to feel that fucking   a runaway train speeding thru me
                              from nowhere headed to no place
                              dropping cargo along the way
was i just cargo?
were we ever friends?
do you tell people we made love or
remember
i
knew
your
mother
ate
food
she
had
prepared   celebrated
birthdays with you   new years   the people we were becoming

progressive language   afrika   red blk & green

i saw you naked
& naked

you were none of these
& me?
i should have screamed kicked slapped fought & been righteously indignant
i should have remembered what my mother never forgot
to tell me
she said: pick up an iron bar   a stick   your fist   whatever!
use whatever you got girl
& fight!

but my strength betrayed me that nite
it ran behind pain 20 years old
& hid

it hid like nazis hide in the argentine dusk
it hid like america hides   behind hollywood, prisons & the right 2 vote
it hid like date rapists hide
at basketball games
& sweet 16's
at pg movies
& in bodegas
at macys & in coffee shops
on the "A" train
uptown &
in brooklyn
in your house
in my house

every 1.3 minutes a woman is raped
which means every 80 seconds a woman is raped
which means every time you hear the first part of this poem
a
woman
has
been
raped
& who knows that woman?
do you know that woman?
do you call that woman, ask advice of that woman?
do you watch that woman,

see her as she dances on torn feet to foreign drums?
do you listen to her poetry beat their tears out on swollen tongues?
do you hold her thru nites that fall like wite phosphorus
onto screaming skins?
& do you walk with that woman
as she visits the morning
& whispers in the ears of trees
& looks for freedom   yes!
oh that woman
she looks for freedom
everywhere!

* *Mumia abu-Jamal, a former Black Panther and journalist (called the "voice of the voiceless") was framed in 1981 for the murder of a policeman who was beating Jamal's brother. He is currently on deathrow in Pennsylvania.*

Rape statistics are from Critical Conditions: Women on the Edge of Violence *(City Lights Books, San Francisco, 1993)*

in response 2 a brother's question about what he should do when his best friend beats up his woman

snatch him up by the back of his neck run him into his own fist
twice
tell him who the real enemy is show him
make him swallow his own teeth do not help when they scratch the inside
of his throat   tell him it was his fault u did this
make his eyes swell up & pus so he looks like a freak   make him go to
work like that & have to come with excuses to his co-workers & friends
tell him the witeman made u do it   tell him you're sorry   tell him u
love him   tell him u didn't mean to then   kick his ass again
Question him on why he's such a coward
Interrogate his ass
Make him beg for forgiveness   Watch him crawl
Put The Word Out In The Streets....
THERE'S AN ENEMY IN OUR PRESENCE THERE'S AN
ENEMY IN OUR PRESENCE   IT DOES NOT THINK IT ONLY
ATTACKS   IT MAKES WEAK-ASS EXCUSES IT TAKES NO
RESPONSIBILITY   IT PICKS ON PEOPLE SMALLER THAN
ITSELF   IT READS SHARAZAD ALI
IT WORSHIPS MILES DAVIS   IT DESTROYS BLKLIFE
IT LIES IT LIES

and if he finally understands
then go to him
find out where it started
search for burn marks beneath his flesh
peel back his pain
be a brother a real good brother
whisper haki madhubuti   sonia sanchez in his ear
sing sweet honey songs
let him cry
let him sleep in your arms
stand alone if u have to
this is the right thing to do
let others babble hate while u break centuries of vicious cycles

face the contradictions the bellies sliced open & jaws wired shut
the assholes torn &
the bloodied vaginas
this is what it looks like do not turn away now
babies beat out of wombs spines curved uneven legs that no longer walk
dead eyes that cannot see tomorrow   livers imprinted   with callused feet—
face the contradiction that looks like u that smells like u
that tastes like u
& push out the violence be unafraid to be a man
who confronts men about women
be unafraid to a man who confronts big small mean common nasty
everyday men
about women
be unafraid to be a man
who confronts
himself.

body-n-soul

i didn't mean for my towel to drop or to be standing nude in front of the
full length mirror the other morning...but there we were, trapped,
the three of us: me, the mirror and my naked body.

i've avoided being nude in front of myself for years...i have hated my
body for nearly as long as i've had one
i've been a million different sizes in my life, but never quite the right size...
my skin was never quite the right shade...
always too light or too dark depending upon
who i was with.

it's not as though i don't know better...
i'm embarrassed to know as many theories as i do
and still be in struggle.

i know that the american aesthetic is perverse, anti-woman
and bounded by a solely western sense of beauty...i know
that even americans did not demand this image of prepubescent fragility
in women until well into this century... i know the
wideness of my hips makes biological sense...
and i know a million other feminist theories and truths....
i have books filled with highlighted paragraphs to prove that i have studied
and
understand these self-affirming things...but that knowing doesn't change
the way i've felt for at least the last 15 years.

i am ashamed to say that i hate my body
but it has been my enemy for so long now
& i know somewhere that the real enemy has been the various reactions
that my body has created in other people who have their own
issues biases agendas & afflictions
but it's easier to attack my 5'6", lightskinned, 142 pound frame...
i have no power over the men who pay me/my body attention
i never wanted
or dispelled affections i desperately needed...
depending upon my state of fatness or thinness....

but this body which is mine, i can
stairmaster
diet, jog, powerwalk and starve into submission.

i don't want to live this way.

i want to see the value of my body in the creative framework of what it
does despite its conformity or non-conformity to the western tradition
i want to value the body i have which has always been able to hold and
to love
to dance, walk, write poems, clean houses, massage my sister, rise every
morning and
try try try
to contribute to another life,
which like mine,
is struggling for something we hesitantly call
peace

poem 4 audre lorde

with love

sometimes i still c u
blkunicorn
riding the edge of the wind
head tilted upward
& eyes speaking deliberate truth
u
were
the last one
who should have left us audre
us   your angry children
                      disguising our silence
                      with our boom boom   our hip hop
                      our gangsta lyrics & gunshot thots
that shred our souls into a million pieces of erased history
that chokes in the throats of our mothers
the ones who left us a legacy of honor we do not serve
with our current retrograde labor
that leaves us all
everyone
blind   broken   begging
from the quietest space in our souls for
real poetry!!
real music!!
real art!!
real culture!!
real real blkpeople whose lives are testimonials
proving....!

WE'RE MORE THAN TRIGGER FINGERS
ON ISRAELI-MADE SUB MACHINE GUNS

WE'RE MORE THAN I BEAT MY BITCH WITH A BAT

we're even more than fly-ass synthesized sounds & drum machines

we're *live* music
big oversize bass muthfuckas
we dimensional   we deep
we complicated coltrane configurations that only God understands

we got things to say
relevant points to make
urgent issues to raise
Audre!

come back
in whatever form u choose
& remind us of us
in us
remind us of the last poets
in us
remind us of the sonia sanchez the gwendolyn brooks the zora neale
hurston the margaret walker the lucille clifton
in us

remind us of the james baldwin the paul laurence dunbar the
langston hughes the claude mckay the haki madhubuti the larry neal
in us

& then the sapphire
in us
the high priest
in us
the jasiri the letta the medina   the baraka
in us
& the voodoo rain
in us
the boyz on the boulevard
in us

audre   remind us of the homegirl in us
remind us of the steel drum   the conga   the 3 chord mississippi piano
(da-da-da-da)
oooh deep feelin muddy waters way down low in big mama thornton
throaty blues
in us
the ball & chain
in us
the *yeah*, come on & rock me baby all nite long
in us
remind us of the freedom codes in slave songs
in us
remind us of the movement
in us
the toi-toi   the capoeria   the lindy   the last dance   the float-like-a-
butterfly-sting-like-bee   200 meter dash   long distance run   black
                            star
                            express   reach
             out & touch
somebody's
hand
in us
& then the science
in us
the social progression & sincerity
in us
Audre!
remind us of the you
in us
remind us of the universe
in us
remind us
the universe is in us
the
universe
is
us
!

chapter two

i write this love poem in blood

love poem, american style

& if the whole world existed inside the love i feel 4 u
then
this poem would be written in the 2 a.m. sands
of south carolina beaches
on paper made of shooting stars
& the rhythm would be a
straight up steel
pulse
beat on
the harmony of *oh lord you make me feeeeel*
baby

if the whole world tasted as pure as u
then i could run my tongue across the earth
as tho it was yr/chest   drink
in the seas like i was drinking in u
& this poem would have entire verses
dedicated
2 yr/arms so
blk/so strong always
holding me
no matter what the distance
btwn us
yeah

if the whole world existed inside
the love i feel 4/u
within the passion u bring forth
then we move as lovers were meant 2 move:
in constant peace
w/nature
w/ready smiles
w/dreams we
can touch

but this is america
& we run hard most
often in the thick mist of broken
spirits haunting the midnite lives crying
for freedom
from hands that condemn blkbabies
with impunity
while lonely mothers sob in the womb
for their disappeared loves   yes

this is america
& children seeking knowledge find only
teenage mutant ninja turtles 4 guidance
while sad-eyed grandparents
generations wise
are discarded
& ignored   yeah

this is america &
gunshots sound more normal than
i love u baby   i really
love
u
in my hometown the persistent rumor is that in 20 yrs all blk/males
                    16-25
                    will have experienced jail

& tonite
as i touch yr/brown
carved
face
twisted
in pain that visits &
does not
leave
i know all my love
is not enough in
a world of traded in
souls

where
maximum profit margin
can be used 2 justify
any amount of killing   i know
in this world
of
Afrikans
& of americans

i write this love poem in blood
i write this declaration of war

from the center 2 the edge

brother
if i had the time
& u had the inclination
i would wrap my tongue
around yr/tears
swallow them   taste u
in places u had traded away
i'd reclaim them 4 u
love u back thru the years   back
into yr/gawky long-armed teenaged days   back
into yr/boyhood   into
yr/mother's belly
if that's where it started
i'd let u be born again
into the promise of
a world that does not grieve its color
i'd liquify yr/pain
throw it past the wind
let my eyes be a mirror
u see yr/self in
& u would see yr/self
like i see u: a wide eyed would-be prophet of the urban nite
sketching fancy dreams
on cheap paper

yr/words are tricks
new-age illusions
i might have believed
but dead birds fell out yr/mouth
when u tried to talk
& i knew...

2.

when we first began
what else mattered

but the orgasms u brought
riding me thru the california morning
on magic afrikan carpets
so often & so good
i refused to challenge the child u were masquerading
as a full grown man

every 3 months
like a bizarre death ritual
u tell me how u hate yr/self
& what words can a woman who's always loved you
say to comfort
that my actions have not shown?

i came to you without armour
never imagining that
u would see love like the razors of yr/mother's screams
like the cheap wine of yr/father's addiction
like the paled eyes & torn mouth of a small boy who tried to suckle milk
out of concrete

what can i tell u now
defined, as u are,
by experiences you refuse to acknowledge
or confront
or survive
or learn from
or get past
or be transformed by
or shake off
or do anything
but keep running
forever if u could
running
a million miles on a tread mill
running

from the center 2 the edge
running
first thing in the morning last thing at nite
running
from eyes that long to reflect in u
the best in u
running
the best in u
is always
running.

4 zayd / absences

in yr/absence
my fingers
b
come
yr/
mouth
exploding
b
tween
my legs
as
insistent
as this
late evening
moon
claiming its
quiet place
crying over
brooklyn
or else
like the
electronic lock
slamming u away
after the
11:00
count

brooklyn was a haiku series
in the summer of '95

a series of torn
cities inside another
where then is my home

you could see the smell
& it was death riding low
down a babbling street

screaming nigga go
home while hissing lemme get
some of that ass first

black bitch / keep walkin'
up my block 10 times but still
i can't find my house

i'm not homeless but
there really is nowhere that
i feel i can live

so what if it is
a cliche where else is it
hotter than bklyn

in summertime and
winter even / my eyes sweat
though once heat could soothe

pores / give life /   it   was
craved & i crawled to it   /   now
i only feel burns

in the space between
my breasts i'm reminded of
your omnipresence

what changed

don't feel no way clear
these days i seek fast exit
into abstraction

no beginnings no
endings no beat no breath no
nothing but i see

loneliness all the
years of love & marriage still
loneliness defines

i can't shake terror
from my eyelids force feeling
back into my hands

i ache to recall
red silk living ... the sound of
color where'd it go

??????

lately the off white
dust of prisons occupy
spaces in my dreams

used to your massage
now i twitch while steel finger
nails scrape at my viens

when i sleep they prick
emotions i can't name &
a death warrant looms

nothing went as planned

brooklyn remember
how you had all the swagger
a black girl needed

you were the heartland
of america to me
you could represent

yeah represent yo!
i loved you fully so how
could you leave me here

crumbling in my prime
watching you wander out the
backdoor of my soul

i took off alla
my clothes & danced naked in
the orange of sunrise

shadows of hunger
played across my stomach &
i let you kiss me there

open mouth pulling
desire out of whispers
i had never known

i would have crawled
you had only to ask / me:
ready on my knees

brooklyn where are your
arms your sinew the back i
once leaned against free

without restraint or
embarrassment i needed
you & you left quick

like you had come in
shadows without proof that you
had ever been here

you went the way of
the irreverent lovers of
my disjointed youth

no future plans or
last names just like both my un-
willing grandfathers

only pain & hard
questions scattered in rooms where
you marked my body
                              brooklyn

how can i survive
you except hate you away
or haiku you gone

                    ?

him

i waited out day / for nite to come with its moon & masquerade of
stillness/where i cld fit my body within the tracings of its own shadow &
just be who i wuz: a cancer woman born/with scorpio on the rise/all water
pouring/emotion/dangerous & free over warnings

i let/okay/i encouraged/you to taste each part of my offerings/not sacrificial
but sacred nonthless/slow   deliberate meeting/your every motion/in train
stations on countertops/you flowed   i followed/til that day i reached
in pathetic futility &   you   were   gone/Lord

my teeth went numb the moment/i realized i wuz unable to feel you
exquisite/at the pulsing of my flesh/open   willing

there were so many changes battles departures/in the 9 - 5 i can't/believe i
survived them all with my dignity/in relative tact/even with you/i just
made a joke as i pulled my boots on/& walked away/& in the aftermath i
have/left no charming messages on your voicemail no beautiful letters or
cards no outreach thru mutual friends/just this poem/alone/still.../your
leaving sears like a branding iron at the core/my God!/of me/i think i really
loved you/in the place where the sun engages the hills & highrises
simultaneously/i used to stand there/watching dreams along lake merrit til
the sky/ came awake/5 am is a forever time i embrace as it stretches the
length/of every muscle/in the same way you did/once/when we started
hesitant   hungry/in the days even the air sighed relief cuz they didn't kill
Mumia/& after that long cold summer framed/by cesspools of executioners
& morticians finally/i could see past the august date with death &/on into
the color of September/ & out of all those dramas hurtings asphyxiations
out of everything what i remember/most about that time is i had all this
love stored up in me like antique & perfect lace dresses locked up in
attic trunks/needing desperately to be worn/once more
that's
what
i tried
to
give
you

in every rose & purple blue iris/in every massage long talk thorough laugh
&/mmm sweet oldtime country fucking/i was trying to say you deserve to
loved in a whole a complete a defining way/& for a long time after it wuz
over /i thought i had to be me/wrong not possessing that thang you know
they say/a woman gotta have to hold a man but now i know this one's on
you/all alone you/go reach back long/to the place where your
movement first began when your back would arch/vainly/into its own
beauty without restraint denial or deprivation its/you/baby/you gotta
learn
how to dance
again.

4:15 in the a.m. / a jailhouse luv story

you enter from a door across the room
steady walk
caribbean confidence &
a hint of an 80s bop
your smile
parading ahead you like a victorious soldier
is a lie.
there is no reason to smile here in the land of confiscated dreams
plastic plants
state-issue clothes
roaches
murder &
blackmen.

i rise to meet you
hold you /
& we lock, perfectly together, like found pieces of a lost puzzle.
we stand like this for 45 seconds, but no longer.
longer might mean a police will come over or yell on the p.a. system:
NO EXTENDED EMBRACES!! EXTENDED EMBRACES ARE A
VIOLATION! RESIDENTS WILL BE WRITTEN UP!

you run your hands through my hair, ask me perfunctory questions:
how wuz the ride up?
did you sleep okay last nite?
can we get business out the way first?
still
luv
me
baby
?

i never sleep the nites before i come to see you
all these years later & i still can't relax
i read
watch television

fantasize
masturbate
but at 3:00 i'm always wide awake waiting for the alarm.
4:15 in the a.m. it'll beep
& i'll shower, drink coffee, figure out what to wear, wait for the van
say a prayer.

you look so pretty today you whisper past my ear
& something inside me shrinks away from your words
i wonder if you mean i looked shitty the last time
& you can't believe i really hooked myself up
this place makes me hostile, defensive, mean & scared
the truth is these crackers could keep you forever
or more likely
they'll find a way to damage you forever
what have i taken on i wonder
but don't say

it's easy to love in 6 hour intervals,
twice per month.
it's easy to love without bills to pay,
responsibilities to share.
in this institution that is rank with the bizarre & vicious odor of
    annihilation,
we have only ourselves to hold up as light and possibility

and i hold you up & i hold you in as
people tell me i am crazy,
loving you across barbed wire & time
but i believe in our love because you struggle with me
lean close to my words,
respect our differences,
honor my mind,
challenge my ideas,
think i can make qualitative change in the lives of our people.
you

take me
real muthafucking serious.

we talk about your case, the one against the state,
where some cracker police set you up with drugs
& had you thrown in the box.
convicts are the easiest people to frame.
who believes a convict or these days
even thinks they are human?
but we thank God for the arrogance and stupidity of police.
they couldn't even do this simple shit right
& you proved it was a lie.
now you just wonder how much the state will have to pay you.
now i just wonder why this is relevant.
10 or 10 million or all the money in the world,
you'll still be in prison.
i'll still be in pain.
i suppose in a broad, political sense
a case like this has serious implications,
but sitting here beneath the shadow of your eyes
& the haunting of our future,
i am narrowed & confined to my own sorrow & needs.

i luv you momi
you say & pull me into a kiss
this type of thing has taken getting used to for me
public affection was never my thing
& as much as i need the insistence of your tongue, part of me numbs
knowing we can be seen.
these crackers & i mean
the black & puerto rican ones too
have unlimited entry into our intimacy & what does that mean?
it means
we are their porno
          their 16mm 2-minute flash of the kinky & forbidden.
we're their gyrating bitches in revolving cages on 8th avenue in n.y.c..
we're their filthy talk on a coffee break

          we are the   dirty joke.

stop it
i say.
let's get back to our discussion.
in a minute momi
you insist
& pull me back into your mouth.
your fingers brush my nipples & i moan
don't do that, & my voice is stunted
& separated from the rest of my body, an exposed nerve pulsating
desire.
after all
i need you too.

your eyes are on the police now,
sitting at the desk.
he's eating a foul-smelling sandwich from the vending machine.
we are shielded by a pole
& your hand slides down my belly, down between my legs, pushes them
apart,
pulls my panties to oneside all in one motion.
in spite of myself,
i am wet.
i
am open &
this could be two lovers at a restaurant,
a movie,
a dinner party,
an office.   this could be sexy / exciting
a memory to cherish   a knowing glance   a private grin
this could be a scene from your favorite erotic movie but instead it is prison.
the sweat is from fear not lust or raw pleasure.
in 20 years we will not remember these as
the hazy crazy bold days of youthful sex.
we will remember what we risked.
we will remember that if we were caught
i would have to visit you through glass for at least a month maybe two,
however long they think it will take til we learn the lesson:
suppress everything you are
have been

will be.
no love
no passion
no hunger
no sensuality
no connection
no bonding
no humanity   no humanity NO HUMANITY NO HUMANITY!

you murmur
oh momi your pussy is so sweet
baby you feel so good
goddamn i need to make love to you....

your fingers on my clit are magic brown butterflies.
i try to be still but cannot stop myself.
i
        shift.
moan.
almost come out my seat.
& i am the rapid waters of the delaware now.
i am the mississippi river,
the amazon,
the nile.
i crave you.
thirst you.
love you.   love you deeply.
i love you like Isis loved Osiris.
& like Isis,
when we are separated,
i spend my days searching for pieces of you
in soweto havana sanfrancisco bedstuy.
i pull these broken parts of you together from corners of the earth
stitched in blood.

i cum
unbelievably
in the warmth of your hands.
the police are still eating

the other visitors & prisoners are still locked
in their own discussions
embraces
cardgames & arguments.
the world is the same.
except for me.
i have changed,
once again,
i
have
changed.

chapter three

a house 2 replace this house

1980-1990, a poet's personal review

1982
and
i
was a
15 yr/old junkie
waste
falling off the edge
of new worlds
& each day
who knew we would live
past 21?
glassy-eyed
teenaged
philosophers   we were
blk & fearless
i hated ronald reagan
republicans
living at home
&
me

moving in a small
unarmed
youthful
army
thru washington square
central park
anyplace
in new york where
you could dare to be different
& stoned

first priority
              yo
              who got the get high?
sensemillia

cocaine
mescaline
& mushrooms

washington d.c.
was a horrible city to live when i moved there
dry
& dull
bougie
boppin to a planet rock beat
the only herb you could
find was soaked
in embalming fluid
nasty shit
we smoked anyway
& love
came with desperation   we both dug reggae & al jarreau
but we screwed to sexual healing
everybody was doing it — trying
to find fantasy in a marvin gaye song
i never did have an orgasm back then
or even learn how to fake it
but it felt good to be held & i took what i could
& stored it away
like a prophecy
of what was
to
come   the 1980s

that decade fell on us like napalm
& we traded love & humanity for pork bellies
on the stock exchange floor while police officers renewed their vows
as klansmen
i was 16
& kids like me hid
themselves away
inside private journals & suicide pacts
cause they seemed like the only real things

in an unreal time
when junk bonds
could be worth millions & human life
worth nothing
&
no
one
talked
about africa
at howard university
where i was a student
girls in my dorm demanded i stopped playing my
wite people
music
they'd
never heard
of bob marley
then
i
guess
& couldn't explain
instead i just got a walkman for christmas
& kept on stepping   blurred

some years are blurred
ugly images
flashing on a screen
i think they made another devil movie
that year
whatever
reagan was re-elected
along with jesse helms
who got 13% of the blkvote   proving
if you starve a man long enough
he will eat anything
including
his
pride

things moved so quickly
!
life was a sound bite
negative campaigning
a 30-second spot
leaving no time to care for this disease
after all its only killing faggots & junkies
& even
blk
americans
didn't
make
the
connection
that it was killing
sober
heterosexuals
in africa
too
til it was
too late
& our own dead babies
began tearing into our dreams
as surely as they defined our
nitemares

& while all this was going on
america murdered maurice bishop
& shit on
grenada
lebanon
libya
the gaza strip
soweto
el salvador
nicaragua
panama
puerto rico
harlem

brooklyn
anywhere
where there were people
trying to make progress

while all this was going on
native americans remained captured
in concentration camps
called
reservations

in
short

these were very sobering times
& even i had to abandon the drugs
since it was
impossible
not to realize
being blk
necessitated
being
alert
being a woman
doubled that
necessity
Tawana Did Tell The Truth!
& it was verified
by a world full of blk women
who's fear kept us
silent
but who's experience
was mirrored
in the eyes of that little girl's face

terror stricken
sprawled
like the venus hottentot
naked for wite

male
perversion

the 1980s
yeah
it was the decade of excess
the media said
but they never did get past donald trump long enough
to tell the truth
excess of racism
sexism
dollarism
excess of wite privilege
excess of blk poverty vomiting
the american dream
on
homeless streets
men
women
children
laid out
like yesterday's garbage
& we stepped over them like
a crack in the sidewalk or
dogshit

still

very few
were talking
revolution

some students stormed their campus'
crying
MONEY FOR SCHOOLS NOT FOR JAILS
which held more blk boys than college classrooms did
wolfpacks
we were told our children
were animals

& they were cut down as such
in that year
that
horrible
horrible
year
when death came hard
& fast
at the hands of blk children
who'd never been taught nuthin
but how to hate themselves
& each other

from january to december
i lived in a funeral home
that held tiny caskets
for babies
our
babies
real
babies
babies who'd had hopes &
dreams &
thoughts &
names
they had names!

       shinnique brown
       veronica corales
       shamel knight
       pierre la rouche
       laykama taylor
       kareem sanders
       leviticus mitchell
       alvin rivera
       sharon shadou
       john thomas jones
       kimson russell
       wilbur pollack

&

this list
is not
complete

this list is not
complete

& even nelson mandela
public enemy
krs-1
afrikan medallions   dreadlocks
kufes
& kente kloth
did not save
these children & some of us
began to wonder if
afrika
& revolution hadn't become
saleable items
symbols
which could be bought
or sold
on any street corner
to anybody
for the right
price   a fad maybe
exchangeable
for a job
(with pension)

keep the faith
we said once as high school seniors
in 1982
keep the faith
we say today but also
we got to do
our

work
blk
people despite difficulty
& circumstance
evil can't be done forever
america will pay for its
crimes
what goes around really will
come around
& we do reap
what we sow if not
for ourselves
then for future generations
eastern europe will eat itself up in its new found capitalism
mislabelled
democracy
while ancient civilizations
the ones
value-based
in humanism
will rise
again

if we do our work
blkpeople
we
will
prevail

poem 4 the students at the city university of new york who questioned why we need 2 struggle

b
cos
if we don't fight
they will kill us
anyway
& then regurgitate
the sweet rhythms
of our grandmother's
voice
in
2
a
funkystank
broken chord of
english only

& it is true that
if we maintain
a warrior-like
unwillingness
2 compromise a
salsa
inspired
soul
that they may fail us everytime
in those
backward
remedial writing
classes
but

so what
if they fail
us
?
!

all them
wite-sounding
puerto rican politicians
in
nyc
still didn't
find the words
2 keep
massive
toxic
garbage incinerators
out the
bronx
or brooklyn
&
what do u say
in
any
language
to
assuage
a sista
who's been
forcibly sterilized
?
!
& which one of

those
so-called
multicultural masturbation certificates
they call
associates degrees
gets u job
that pays the rent
&
buys enough
food
!

& if we don't start it up move it along
make some noise
then
those of us who know
will never convince
those of us
who don't know
that nat turner harriet tubman geronimo pratt lolita lebron haydee torres
were
&
are
real
brown skins & hearts & lungs
shoving
death
back
in
2
the faces
of those
who
made the earth a concentration camp
& sold children
& beat pregnant women in ditches
& who now claim apartheid was a necessary evil
& who
lied & revised &

murdered
everybody everybody everybody
who offered them
friendship
in strange lands
i mean
we got to show
that
coloredfolks
can & do fight
can & do win
not some heavyweight wite-run bullshit boxing battles
but
2
the
death
battles
preserve
blklife
battles
honor the earth
battles &
if we don't battle
what will do

?

find satisfaction in being
tokenized
on recruitment posters of chemical corporations
designed 2 market disease & destruction
2 our very own babies
while our heads
are wrapped up
tight
in small print forms
that contract our lives
away
what

will
we
do
?
?
?
run
circular around
gucci shoes
&
watches
maybe 2
car garages
or afrikan vacations taken
on european travel plans
watching
the ashanti
the zulu
the fulani
the ga
from safari convoys
waving a flag
singing

            hey   sing it loud
        i'm american &
            proud
        ???????
& our whole lives
will surely dissipate
& then disintegrate
in
2
dusty museums
where in
10 yrs   in
20 yrs   in
50 yrs
little wite children will read
pretty printed signs

that
say:

THESE WERE THE COLORED PEOPLE
KILLED OFF BY CAPITALISM & COMPLACENCY
ILLEGITIMIZED BY IMPERIALISM & INDIFFERENCE
ANNIHILATED BY AMERICANISM & APATHY

& apathy
& apathy
& apathy
& apathy

on the way out of san fransisco
i wrote this poem

within our desperate attempts
at liberation
i watch the faces of my teachers
as they crumble
like stale bread
beneath
the heavy hand of madness
& self deceit
exhaustion
& distorted rationales
that leave us
wandering
& aimless
along familiar paths of backward repetition
ignoring the lessons
of our
dead whose
dying
brutal
& premature
will remain
unavenged
as we give in
to old tricks
that keep us
murdering & murdered
engaging & engaged
in futile battles
of who will be the biggest nigga
in the yard
of wite supremacy

politically correct language
& recitals of current progressive theory
only proves
that we can read
& report on what we read
but alone
is no testimonial
to our
humanity

together
we comprise
a staggering
lonely army whose similarities
are no longer
love & liberation
but ritual abuse
that winds like a viper into the fresh blood
of
our
beloved

broken soldiers
we
are   still
determined
tho we constantly lose our
footing trying to
heal a world
before
healing ourselves
first

and so

we scream
we rant
we bear witness after
heartbreaking witness
to the atrocity that is america
yet justify
ourselves
as we beat
our lovers
our children
our mothers
our fathers

we curse the weakness of uncle toms and
turncoats
but excuse our own desertions
of our families and friends

and i am a woman
a student of revolution
who loves deeply the spirit
of my people
still
my pain
twists
and multiplies
in unforgiving
succession
as the living symbols of our strength
reduce themselves into common jail house gangsters
who pardon the rape of young black boys or

empty headed cowards who direct their blackfists
of power
upon the faces of their women

or else women–
women who can only survive by chewing at the flesh
of their very own sisters

picking bare their bones
erasing their names

and others still
who hide their meaning behind liberation colors
in order to steal the energy
the affection
the trust
of sacred communities of people of colors
only to fuck it all away
in european beds

and this poem has no ending

no answer to give you   only us
willing ourselves into collective metamorphosis   us
gathered together, critically   sincerely   us
only   us
and   only   then

a change gon come
ooohhh yes
*ooohhh yes it will**

*sung by sam coooke

truth

for Haki Madhubuti

filtering out life
like the sands of an eroding beach
       blown/shifted
washed up -n- away
new york
atlanta

soweto
kingston
eurocentric dust storms inhibit our
onward motion   our
upward movement

who r we
?

surely not puppets
surely not evil
surely not undeserving

foster homes wic checks leather bombers roaches
public schools turned 2 prisons
prisons turned 2 housing developments 4 the poor
reality check
(1-2 what is this?)

what this is
is lonely mothers and lost fathers
lost mothers and lonely fathers
scattered children everywhere
here
what this is
is america
our america
black america

dismayed
dissolved
disassembled &
deceived

honored among us r oversized ballplayers
who pimp $200 sneakers 2 wide-eyed babies
who have never known an adequate meal

honored among us r red-black & green freaks
who yell BLACKPOWER
while reducing el-hajj malik
2
a
letter
in
the
alphabet

honored among us r nuclear shitting black generals
who build their careers on the graves of black babies
while proclaiming
i'm not black i'm not white i'm just the color of my uniform
douglas macarthur never said no shit like that
he knew what side he was supposed 2 be on!
why
don't
we
?

bmw's   2-finger rings   gold nameplates
          "yo baby i got the nice nice product"

tell no lies
mask no difficulties
claim no easy victories

no matter where they invest their money
drug dealers r genocidal muthafuckers selling death 2 our people
& our silence convicts each one of us
at their trials
& their r no appeals 2 be made
at a funeral parlor

in egypt
blackmen r selling off pieces of the pyramids in order to pay their rent
in san francisco
my sista was forced 2 choose between her children or going to a protest
that might
save their lives
in palestine
hatem, 7
exchanged his childhood for the return of his nation
and in new york
20,000 afrikans r buried under federal buildings and courthouses
while above ground
black people receive lifetime bids
dealt out in 6 month sentences
in 2 year sentences
in 5 year sentences
and somebody said
all you need is love
but what does love got 2 do
got 2 do
got 2 do
with it
when love has become a political tradewind
always changing direction
& degree

where r the forever people
where r the word-is-bond people
where r the people of integrity
where r the people who promised...
???

we rise & pray daily
while unattended scriptures
choke on the gathered dust of our own hypocrisy
porkchop preachers who can organize press conferences but not people
must be reminded
that nat turner was their father
and words without action is only noise &
cannot &
will not
& does not
save the lives
of our
brown babies
save the lives of our
brown babies

no turn backs

c my people
dressed in black
u know we come a long way
& we ain't turnin back
wade in the water
wade in the water children
wade in the water
u know my God is gonna trouble these waters 4 me
until all Afrikan people are free

what distinguishes this nite is the silence
falling e-z around my shoulders
a short lived pretense
2 peace
& its not that i'm unappreciative
it's that i'm aware

> *fast moon setting &*
> *the morning comes*
> *bringing with it statistics*
> *that do not lend themselves 2 metaphor...*

oh
& if i could
i would write luvpoems all day
burn incense
watch my candles glow
tell u stories of only beauty
but such choices r not mine
2 make
when the times have demanded of me
this ritual: the laying out of funeral clothes
                                the loss of another blkchild

gone   too   soon
& now
now we walk

heads bowed
in a world of neutralized people

                                    blkfaces of stone
who no longer allow themselves
2 feel
& so they lie
they lie about everything 2 everybody
& dismiss the eruption of afrikan volcanoes spitting maroon lava
like its some freaky side show:

                          can't u write anything else
                          asha
                          ?
                          doesn't anything make u happy
                          ?

baby   they   don't   know
i have a range of emotion
& i wanna be yr/lifetime smile
i wanna make luv 2 u past the midnite
ride yr/passion into the frenzied dawn
tease yr/sweat into necessary water

4 us 2 swallow
whole
&
complete
& then make u
ease &
arch

& stretch   baby
i
mean
i
need
2

make
u
feel

but touch is not a simple thing
nor does it come without a past   (a present)
& we
we poets/blk
& in desperate
luv
with people & possibility
we poets/blk & splitting moods & winning awards & publishing books
we
poets
blk
will remain in   u-n-d-i-s-r-u-p-t-e-d pain
since we are apparently without even 1 word
within all these fancy/hip words
that can birth justice
as quickly as america buries it
we poets/blk
are reaching & clawing & trying
we poets   we're crying our words
& searching our worlds
4 a place 2 build a new house
a house 2 replace this house   this house   this house (!)
cuz this is the house that greed & historical revisionism built
this is the house that blk/grandmothers shot dead in they own kitchens
& witeboys walked free built
this is the house that
middle passages
blanketed diseases
the pearl river
bloody new jersey turnpikes
counter intelligence
napalm
nuclear wipeouts of entire peoples
skull & bones
contras   vietnam iraq grenada

unconditional aid 2 israel
atlanta 1979
puerto rico 1898
death row/mumia   falsified evidence
marion federal penitentiary
drug czars
3 strikes u out
&
southern
trees
bear
strange
fruit.
blood on the leaves
& blood on the root
black bodies swinging
in the southern breeze
strange fruit hanging
from the poplar
*trees**
&
wite
boys
walked
free
built

this is the house that roy innis built
this is the house that absolute hatred built
& silence & individualism & the appointment of clarence thomas
sanctioned
this is the house where blkgirls could be so exhausted by 16
that they'd whisper 2 me

listen asha
i don't care about nuthin   i
just wanna live
okay
?

behind the steady succession of assaults
used 2 be warriors trade in the truth 4 loot
(gotta gotta get some loot yo!)
& we don't even reach 30
anymore
b4 giving up
or else giving out
our energy
2 any palefaced freak

who would replace our sun
with neon
& who would replace us!
us builders & dreamers &
dragonslayers
& peacemakers
with dead eyed
rhythmless
stupefied
zombie yes men
who stumble thru the universe
dribbling shit on us & our children
babbling
garbled reagan like sound bite theories
without lite
without luv
without life

written and sung by Billie Holiday

rage

this poem was written as an assignment for us to create a piece about "what we were feeling in the moment," while taking a workshop at the New School. the workshop extolled, solely, the literary expressions of white men, although it wasn't supposed to be a course on white men. the instructor rambled on about how poetic form was revolutionary. i eventually dropped the class, but not before writing this piece.

i wuz thinkin rage which isn't really/this moment
but a cacophony of moments/when i realize what & who propells
me/& a nation of poets past language & into life/will once more be whited
out ignored unimportant undiscussed perhaps a footnote willfully forgotten/
bcuz the new school ain't nuthin but the old school/though i
shouldn't complain since i wuz warned/but i had promised myself
no more shakespeare no more dead witemen over done wite women til i
have read all/every one of the slave narratives/& my eyes scream when i hear
asha god damn this is your last semester just ignore it/but there wuz always
a reason a rationale to ignore my own evaporation/
i can't do it anymore
& i know i'm much more likeable when its all about my miserable drug
addicted whore of a life/but the biggest part of me rages/which
is what i wuz tryin to talk about/cuz i don't give a fuck anymore
about these bizzare *hey lets play word games & make*
abstract meaningless diatribes/that get passed off as poetry when
jayne cortez when marlon riggs when willie perdomo
when tony medina when kevin powell
when devorah major when pat parker when audre lorde when ntozake
shange when pedro pietro should i go on? when piri thomas when wanda
coleman when mari evans
you get the idea
when these poets & the poets who came after them
are yanking death outta peoples walks/
& i mean in a constant way/
what about them who don't believe in poetic form as is/
but form as bridge as shoulder as hand as pull as reach as try as food

as water/
as is as will always be
the real the relevant the required
revolution

blues poem 4 malcolm x

it was some wild shit
that day
& we sat back 4 a moment
paralyzed
our eyes
shock-wide
open like a crazy cartoon   a overstretched caricature
of self
we watched them resurrect you
just so they could kill you
one
mo'
time
again
but   a cat has 9 lives
&

you wuz a big-ass
mean
beautiful
black
cat
          malcolm
          malcolm
          malcolm
listen
some of us still want 2 be
free

potato chips   x-caps   t-shirts   movies
"the only revolutionary is a dead revolutionary"

exposed
disrupted
& otherwise neutralized*

ain't it funny what could happen 4 money?
you couldn't be bought while you wuz alive
but dead & buried
you been straight up
commodified

while we wuz sleepin
someone stole our rage
& sold it back to us in a non-profit government funded
package
& called it
progress

but
malcolm
malcolm
malcolm
listen...
some of us still want 2 be free

& we hear you
crying from inside your grave
screaming as yr/enemies masquerading as friends or else
experts
speak in tongues forked
with lies designed to corrupt
the
straight-backed
blk

honest
movements
of young warriors seeking
only the restoration of
truth
malcolm
listen

in these bizarre days that birth fear from toxic tinged wombs
promoting perversion as normalcy

in these days when centrally unintelligent presidents can march grinning
blksoldiers upon blklands
from california 2 somalia

when blkmayors could drop bombs on blkbabies
take
full responsibility
& be commended by blkpeople even
as we burn   & break   & dissipate

in these days of open f.b.i. agents accepted as preachers of truth
as leaders in some path of righteousness

in these days when the african national congress
could lie down with the dogs of apartheid

& the conscious among us would fight each other more
often than fighting the enemy
& we wind up killing the enemy
b4
realizing
the enemy was
us

malcolm
in these days deliberately directed toward total destruction
do
not
despair
do not let yr/own tears drown you out yr/own grave

some of us still want 2 be free &

even if they chisel yr/face into mount rushmore smiling beside stonefaced
slaveowners

even if they get the blkest blkman alive 2 write a book that says you
really loved crackers

even if mtv flashes yr/image on a ray charles video singing god bless
america

even if they cut you so bad
carve you so deep
that michael jackson has to cringe

malcolm
if they say you never really loved us

some of us will still not be fooled
some of us will still want 2 be free

listen
we beat these blues out on bass drums for what they did to you knowing
we must wail a warchant for what we will do to them

malcolm...
in new york
not all blkyouth seek salvation by shaking our asses & smoking
blunts on friday nites
some of us
study
&
train
&
teach
&
create

& in america
every single political prisoner
is
still
standing firm
in the face of   24 hour

365
sensory depriving
no contact visiting
lock down living
&
STAND
STRIP
LIFT YR/BALLS
TURN AROUND
BEND OVER
SPREAD YR/CHECKS
HANDS ON YR/HEAD
BACK OUT YR/CELL
UP
AGAINST
THE WALL
MUTHAFUCKA!!!!!!!!!!!!

has not
did not
cannot
break the blkbacks of resistance
malcolm!
malcolm!
malcolm!
listen
do not let yr/own tears drown you out
yr/own
grave cause
yeah
some of us still gonna be
free
malcolm
malcolm
malcolm

* *from Hoover's FBI memo regarding the growth of the Black Panthers and the black power movement*

afterword

a prayer for the living

for kimson russell & the spirit of his family

The New York Times (11-30-90):   "... On Thursday, Kimson Russell was supposed to celebrate his 17th birthday ... instead ... Mr. Russell's family and friends will gather for this funeral ... The teenager ... was shot to death on Saturday night on a street corner in the East New York section of Brooklyn ... at least a half-dozen young people have been slain in the area in the last two years ...."

I

a ringing phone & a hushed voice
breaks
the quiet of a sunday morning
> *they shot veberly's son last nite*
> *he's dead*
impossible
i think
i must be in a nitemare
but the voice doesn't go away
& i am awake
awake & calling veb
offering words & thoughts of
support & sorrow
words a mother ought never have to hear
(it is too frightening to ask the necessary question: will this be
> another decade of dead
> children?)

so
we plan this funeral
this memorial
this teach-in
this burial
worrying throughout
there is no money to cover the cost

a friend asks :   but how is a mother ever to have such money?
               how was she supposed to plan for this expense?

we'll have everything right here
veb says
in the community
she says

but its the trenches she means
for this is a war zone

& we are casualties
each one of us
walking wounded
the scars seen
& unseen

II

for kimson russell
taken at 16
for his mother & sister
for his brother & grandmother
for the girl he loved
for the baby he made
for the father he never knew
nor
touched

for all blkpeople
who have buried their children
as unprepared soldiers
in this war   this war   this war
we did not ask for &
cannot seem to escape
this war against blk
this war against blkhumanity
raging on mean mean streets
called

sutter
&
euclid

for all those who have been taken before this day
for all those who will not be saved tomorrow
for all those whom no one remembers
nor who's spirits we honor

i submit this humble prayer
in the name of the mothers & the fathers
the sons & the daughters
the brothers & the sisters
the friends & the lovers

to those of us still living
from this day forward....

      may we walk forever in clarity
      that we shall nevermore confuse
      the enemy from the friend
      nor be organized into gangs against each other
      nor place material before soul
      nor participate in our own murders

      may we walk forever in honor
      because within us lies the reality of who
      we have been
      & who we might be/come

      may we walk forever in strength
      for strength is the legacy of the children
      of the people
      who survived the middle passage

      may we walk forever with pride
      wherever we may travel
      for our ancestors were founders
      philosophers & builders

& they have willed us nothing less

may we walk finally & forever
in peace amongst our people
with respect & with dignity
despite our differences
for it is only us
as brothers & sisters

who can lead us thru these
the darkest
of
days

ashe.

asha bandele,

over the last seven years, has read poetry throughout the United States and southern Africa. Her work can be found in the anthologies *In the Tradition*, *Aloud*, and *In Defense of Mumia* as well as in countless academic and community periodicals.

Since 1990, bandele has taught poetry in prisons, in juvenile detention centers, and in alternative schools. She has been the poet-in-residence for Rise and Shine Video Productions and was the co-coordinator for San Francisco's Black Star Express Poetry and Jazz Night at the Upper Room. She graduated from The New School for Social Research in 1996.

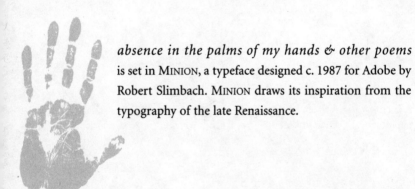

absence in the palms of my hands & other poems is set in MINION, a typeface designed c. 1987 for Adobe by Robert Slimbach. MINION draws its inspiration from the typography of the late Renaissance.